The Number Before Infinity

Also by Zack Rogow

Author
Voices Carved from Obsidian (chapbook)
My Mother and the Ceiling Dancers
Greatest Hits: 1979-2001
The Selfsame Planet
A Preview of the Dream
Make It Last
Glimmerings
Oranges (for children)

Editor
The Face of Poetry
Two Lines: Masks
Two Lines XIV: World Writing in Translation

Translator
Earthlight by André Breton (translated with Bill Zavatsky)
Arcanum 17 by André Breton
Horace by George Sand
Green Wheat by Colette
Marius by Marcel Pagnol

The Number Before Infinity

poems by
Zack Rogow

Copyright © 2008, 2014 by Zack Rogow
All rights reserved
Printed in the United States of America
Second edition, Copyright © 2014 by Zack Rogow

Artwork and cover design by San Francisco-based public mural artist and illustrator Mona Caron / www.monacaron.com

Page design, composition and typography by Dickie Magidoff

Back cover photo by Margaretta K. Mitchell

Published by:
Scarlet Tanager Books
P.O. Box 20906
Oakland, CA 94620
www.scarlettanager.com

Library of Congress Cataloging-in-Publication Data
Rogow, Zack.
    The number before infinity : poems / by Zack Rogow.
      p. cm.
    ISBN-13: 978-0-9768676-0-9 (alk. paper)
    ISBN-10: 0-9768676-0-5 (alk. paper)
    I. Title.
    PS3568.O493N86 2008
    811'.54—dc22
                            2008023653

Acknowledgments

The author wishes to thank the editors who published these poems in anthologies, in magazines, and on web pages.

"1 BR Sublet ½-Frnished" in *poetrymagazine.com*
"A Map of You" in *Greatest Hits: 1979-2001* (chapbook from Pudding House Publications). Anthologized in *Velvet Avalanche: A Collection of Erotic Poetry*
"A Sonnet—Against Regret" in *The Carquinez Review*, and the web site Verse Daily
"B E A C H S T O R M   T A N K A" in *poetrymagazine.com*
"Charged Particles: An Email" in *Switched-on Gutenberg*
"Counting the Years" in *m.a.g.*
"Dogsitting: Twelve Days" in *Facets*
"En Prouvènço" in *sfstation.com*
"First Kisses" anthologized in *All Hail Blue and Gold*
"Flight 000" in *Runes*, and anthologized in *Blue Arc West: An Anthology of California Poets*
"Hilltop Townhouse" in *Floating Holiday*
"How Do You Say 'Jet Lag' in French?" in *Rive Gauche*
"In Bed, With the Shade Up, On a Night in August" in *in*tense*
"Insomnia at the Solstice" in *Revolve*
"Modigliani and You" in *Facets*
"Opening" in *Illya's Honey*
"Outside the Borders" in *m.a.g.*
"Running Away" in *Miller's Pond*
"Skating Lessons" in *Off the Coast*, and anthologized in *Proposing on the Brooklyn Bridge: Poems about Marriage*, and in *Greatest Hits: 1979-2001*
"Snarls" in *Cloud View Poets* (anthology)
"So soft your lips at first . . ." anthologized in *Velvet Avalanche: A Collection of Erotic Poetry*
"Storm at the Rim of the Continent" in *Illya's Honey*
"Symmetron: You and Brother Will" anthologized in *in A Fine Frenzy: Poets Respond to Shakespeare*
"The Number Before Infinity" in *Xanadu*
"Three Ages" in *Facets*

Contents

1.

    3   Opening
    4   "I want to nose your earlobe in Kyoto . . ."
    5   The Number Before Infinity
    6   Carpool
    7   Counting the Years

2.

    11   How Do You Say "Jet Lag" in French?
    12   En Prouvènço
    13   Of All the Gin Joints in All the Towns in All the World, She Walks into Mine

3.

    17   "Maybe it's easier for us to be together . . ."
    19   First Kisses
    20   First Time
    21   "So soft your lips at first . . ."
    22   Safe
    23   "This secret . . ."
    24   Without Ceremony
    25   A Map of You
    26   The Birth of a Heart

4.

    29   "I'm a Lilliputian . . ."
    30   Storm at the Rim of the Continent
    31   BEACH STORM TANKA
    32   Running Away

33 Who to Think To
34 Break in the Weather
35 At Opposite Ends
36 Charged Particles: An Email

5.

39 Skating Lessons
40 Before-the-Divorce Rainboots
41 Beneath a Blue Moon
42 Departure at Chanukah

6.

45 Dogsitting: Twelve Days
46 Insomnia at the Solstice
47 Hilltop Townhouse
48 Flight 000
49 1 BR Sublet ½-Frnshed
50 Turquoise Planets of Your Eyes
51 The Way We Touch
52 You're Not My Daddy
53 Rentals

7.

57 Outside the Borders
58 In Bed, With the Shade Up, On a Night in August
59 I Want You (To Start Taking Me More for Granted)
60 Indulgence
62 Modigliani and You
63 Symmetron: You and Brother Will
64 Exercise
65 A Sonnet—Against Regret
66 Snarls
67 Three Ages
68 Under a Black Lace Sky

Toujours Colette

The Number Before Infinity

I.   ∞

Opening

I'm open so wide
                so wide
I don't have any skin.

Words overheard
on the sidewalk
jostle me left and right. Every breeze
becomes a parade,
every scratch
a torrent.

Even a dancer suddenly   lifted
is enough to lift *me*.

And just a pebble of a country song
rattles my fault lines:
I'm in so deep
Can't think of gettin' out

I'm open so wide
                so wide
to take in each of your glances,
all of your long dark hair.

∞

I want to nose your earlobe in Kyoto
under the stilts of restaurants with lanterns
squiggling in the river
I want your pillowy kisses in Paris
with the Seine flooding your irises
I want to tightrope the edge
of the ocean with you at Point Reyes
as the beach raises your hair
and land in your arms
in a Victorian drawing room searching
frantically for you
amidst the bustles ribbons and taffeta
or feel your hips insistent in a black gondola
in 18th century Venice
with you the man and me the woman this time
on a cool night
in the Israel of Bathsheba and David
I'd like to stroke warm almond oil
into the grooves of your back
to bathe you
in ancient Greece
overlooking coastal blue
exchange robed glances with your eyes
in the Marrakesh market
I'd like to sit next to you
in high school math
and play footsie during trigonometry
I want to love you on a planet
with two suns two moons
and no people
who might blab they saw us
holding hands in public

The Number Before Infinity

Slapping her bath, my five-year-old insists
she wants to count to infinity. "You can't,"
I tell her, "even if you spend your whole life."
"Then what's the number
before infinity?" she asks.

You and I both know the limits—we can think
hopes out loud when we're together
but we can't even say each other's name
in our sleep, lying next to the ones
who made our lives seaworthy.

When our carpool drops you off
and your daughter smiles
at the window, waving hello,
I know when that door
closes behind you, it locks.

You ask a mathematician
my daughter's question about infinity.
"Infinity sometimes behaves
like a number," the professor explains,
"but sometimes it's just an idea."

Carpool

In the back seat
only an arm's length away
I can't reach out
can't even toss glances with you

but when when I stare at the woods
on Mount Tamalpais
I'm thinking of
pushing my hands
up into your closely planted hair

and when I follow the fog
slithering through the Golden Gate
my finger is
silking between your legs:
Come to me

Counting the Years

Before we met I was counting—counting the years
13 before the youngest flies to college
15 since the wedding cake
17 more of mortgage
19 till pension

But if you're counting the years
you're just saying your lines
and every night I stopped
before I turned my key
in the front door
not believing at all
I could make it
till bedtime

The Number Before Infinity

2.

How Do You Say "Jet Lag" in French?

The sun hasn't set in two days.
If I don't drag myself to nightfall
Paris will slip out of my hands. All I can do is sit
on these stone steps by the green Seine
and lick ice cream.
I've got three different colored spheres,
the flavors so concentrated
an entire harvest
has pushed into each of them.
The *framboise* makes me think of you.

On the plane I cried,
even with Paris waiting for me, cried
because every direction was blocked for us.
For a moment I thought I could spot a path,
solid as a scoop of cloud,
but as the aircraft descended
it slit right through.

When I've licked away my *glace* by the Seine
I walk the river to the Sainte Chapelle,
a cathedral in miniature,
where even the king and queen would kneel.

The world inside is all stained glass,
story upon story embedded in lozenges of every color
pouring from ceiling to floor.
This must be what it's like
inside the brain of God
where each scene's trapped in flat black lead
but burns in azure, gold, and red.

En Prouvènço

> *So from one clear and living fountain pour*
> *the sweet and the bitter that I feed upon*
> Petrarch

In the village of Fontaine de Vaucluse in Provence
the River Sorgue surges as if from
nowhere, not by adding up rivulets and rills,
but by spilling the full burden of its current
from the ribs of a canyon,
waterfalls sliding out of the hillside
right under my feet.

By this riverhead Petrarch wrote
one sonnet to Laura
for every day of the year.
He glimpsed her in the Church of St. Clare
in Avignon, her twined brown hair
molten. His lips
never touched hers.

No one has ever traced the source
of the River Sorgue
though robots have plunged
into the cavern it rolls from,
probing with lights,

but the river constantly dives
around rocks and boulders
where lovers perch, the couples
soothed by the
thrashing of the current.

Of All the Gin Joints in All the Towns in All the World, She Walks Into Mine

> *But the others wait in Casablanca—*
> *and wait—and wait.*

I used to hate that line in *Casablanca*
when Ingrid Bergman in her Cubist bonnet
simpers to Humphrey Bogart, "I don't know
what's right any longer.
You'll have to think for both of us . . ."
At that moment she has all the spine
of cookie dough in the oven.

But now I've reached a frame
where I could be playing Miss Ilsa.
Thoughts of you shake me
till I'm a refugee from my own life.
"So now, Meester Reeck, if you don't mind
I'd like those letters of transit, heh, heh."
And I could take all the fundamental things that apply
and ship them straight to hell.

That's why you've got to think for both of us now
and I'm praying you'll choose wrong
since I want a flight to your love
more than I want the beginning
of a beautiful friendship.

The Number Before Infinity

3.

∞

Maybe it's easier for us to be together
since neither of us is single.
We're not starving
so we can taste each kiss
like a chef sipping a dish
before he serves it.
We don't have to worry
if our incomes could
outrun our spending.

On those Sunday nights
when the weekend drains away
like a child's bath,
our homes still stand.
And we don't have to concern ourselves
about tuxedos and lace.

Yes, it's so much easier to be together
since we're both already
with someone else. Of course
when we wave goodbye on the street
we're actually not in our own bodies,
but standing outside ourselves,
kissing. We can only visit Venice as a couple
in a room rippling with eels of light
reflected off the canal
if we close our eyes tight.

And there will never be a child
with your eyes, the blue and green
speckled like a pottery glaze;
with my Mediterranean nose
and your bold chin;
my long fingers
and your thick, dark hair.

First Kisses

The Botanic Garden was moist
from record rains,
branches thick
with tiny purple flowers. Their aromas
trickled up into the air.

We sat on wooden steps
overlooking the canyon
with a view all the way to the bay,
houses spilling up
the hills of San Francisco,
where we live apart.

When you kissed me
I thought of those Flemish Annunciations,
the angel both female and male
with long trills of hair—
your tongue fluttering
but determined.

First Time

Our first night together the sun shone
through the balcony doors.
The bed wasn't mine
and it wasn't yours.

Finally I could scream
your name out loud.
When I cried
out of sheer relief
you licked up the salt tears.
Then I sleeked and wetted you
the way a woman would,
your thighs pressing my ears so tightly.

And you took me
like a man,
your crucial kiss
at just the right time.

∞

So soft your lips at first
like cake frosting

tongues
liquefied
flickering

till our mouths got wider and wilder
we almost swallowed
each other whole

And later when it was all over
and we looked in our eyes
the afternoon
           stopped
and the kisses turned
                  intentional
        each
                                distinct
      and lunar
              as if our hearts
                      were passing
right through our ribs
                      and touched
            every time
   our lips met

Safe

Safe I thought I was safe
just up to my ankles
how could I ever
you ten years
with another
and your child suffering
the shocks of her own brain
each day
I was so sure
I didn't see it
about to break
that first time
at the hotel
the clerk noticed
no car or baggage
I won't ask she said
Go ahead you challenged

I closed the latch the room
hugged a double bed
words leaped out
when we kissed
I don't know how much longer
I can hold back
before I tell you
I love you
And your answer—
Then don't hold back

Our bodies printed our words
onto each other
and I was finally completely
safe

∞

This secret
that we both carry
weighty and glistening
as a carved marble of braided lovers

there's no one
we can consign it to
for even a few minutes
for fear of smashing
everything

No   no one
we can ask
for a blessing
or failing that
for understanding
or at least
a head shaking
both knowing and amused

So we have to lean against each other
and with our hands
smooth into each other
knowing
and understanding
and even a blessing

Without Ceremony

Other couples have ways
of showing their unity—
the vows and bands they trade,
the joint property with pools
of shadow on the lawn,
the infant boys and girls
whose eyes, mouths, and noses
blend their parents' traits.

We have only touch,
the embraces that solder us
when we tear across a rented bed,
our smells that tangle,
and the flicks and rings our mouths shape
when we summon the thunder

A Map of You

You've become my map, my geography:
the Black Forest of your hair,
your alpine lake eyes,
fathom after fathom,
your mouth red as turned Carolina earth,
those shoulders like Dover's
chalk towers, your Sugarloaf breasts,
by your peninsular arms—
Baja,
Malaysian,
and your fingertips
when they touch me—
Polynesian archipelagoes. Serengeti
the temperature of your flesh.
Your Panama waist
flares to Venezuelan thighs
and between them
the Amazon, the delta, rare species
of the Galapagos, coral reefs with ultraviolet fish—
in just a few short months
you've become the other planet I inhabit.

And your legs taper
like a continent headed south,
one ending in Tierra del Fuego—
the Land of Fire—
and the other
in the Cape of Good Hope.

The Birth of a Heart

Yesterday I cried out
how unfair
that we didn't meet before
we had children, before
our lives hardened, before
it became so difficult
for lips to overlap.

But it wasn't on any lover's pillow
that I learned to untwine my heart for you.
It happened minutes after I first became a father
when I chased an incubator into intensive care
where my daughter's doll arms were taped
to keep her from swatting the I.V.
and her tiny heart was punching
at her chest, thin as silk,
and I stood there with absolutely no idea what to do
to soothe her pain
till the nurse said to me,
"Talk to her,
she already knows your voice."

The Number Before Infinity

4.

∞

I'm a Lilliputian
down near the soil. Not the giant
you loved last week
when you wanted
to be buried next to me.

Now you see my ankle stature.
I'm a special effect, I can't play
your leading man.

But will you still pick me up,
hold me in your palm,
take off my doll clothes,
stroke my little head,
and blow off the dirt from the ground?

Storm at the Rim of the Continent

Breakers crumble and moil
as the wind tries to push them back to sea.

A pennant of sandpipers
yanks through the air.

Pelicans hoist themselves
onto the sky. I hike

my coat over my head,
hide from the downpour.

The tide wheels tree trunks
onto the coast, as the ocean spreads

its liquid nets, till it traps
the whole beach this time,

scattering me onto white quartz boulders.
Logs charred to black mosaics

lie skewed next to stranded kelp,
twisted from its bed,

the sand a moonscape marbleized
by the last wave that rinsed it.

BEACH STORM TANKA

I don't crave the tranquility
of a coffee table lake.
Give me that slish and moan
of the shape-changer ocean,
liquid kaleidoscope.

Running Away

When my daughter can't take her parents' shouting,
can't stand the nagging about a bath,
she gets ready to run away.

She packs her favorite teddy bear
whose name is a question: How Are You?
and takes her blanky
with its batting foaming out
and shoves it in her backpack
with a granola bar
and makes a run for the front door.

I panic that she might actually
submerge herself in the night
and disappear somewhere
she can't find her name.

But I know
that she knows
even when she dashes toward the door
she'll never go farther
than the next house. She's aware

our property line forms the edge
of the earth for now
and her parents will always chase
and carry her home.

Am I doing that, too,
sprinting toward another house
just to see who will follow?

Who to Think To

I don't know who to think to anymore.

For so long it was my gold band, my wife.
I talked to her silently
all through our daughter's first year,
marked by the fear
that our child's new brain was scarred
and by her slapstick joy.

And when I could no longer find my wife's ear,
it became you, my turquoise lover,
for one triumphant year
as we grew up together
at time-lapse speed.

And when I gave her up
I lost the "you" in my head,
and now I'm thinking to no one
except the Zen therapist
who shakes off every punishment
I propose for myself
till I reach
for the next tissue,
and clench in my hand
that tiny moon.

Break in the Weather

       between ashen clouds
the sky
         blue as fire
sometimes
                 I catch myself
     still thinking to you

At Opposite Ends

For months we knew
the same morning train moved us,
but at opposite ends.
We stayed apart,
veering from that sidetrack love.
When we both got out at the same stop
my eyes would race
for just a glimpse of you.

Then one day
still travelling in my seat
I wondered if my children
would some day ask me Daddy
who was that woman
you wrote all these poems to?
and I decided to walk the length of the train
to find out.

        Ten crowded cars
and every person had your face.

In the last car I saw you stand up
as I walked down the aisle
and I knew
yours were the only lips
I ever wanted to kiss.

Charged Particles: An Email

As I write this you're running in Chicago for your connecting flight to the East Coast, zigzagging through the strobe light crowd, searching for the silver plane you're already flying on in your thoughts. But you're reading this three days from now back home in San Francisco, your body in multiple time zones, and while you tap on the computer I touch the keys from the other side, like the black reflection the pianist sees over the notes. Actually I'm three days behind you, trying to catch up, I'm whispering in your ever-so-sensitive ear: I can't imagine living without you now. And while your flight unzips the continent this message streams to you in a string of electrons, capillaries of gold lights mirrored in the glass windows of a merry-go-round made up of neutrinos, colored quarks—particles as interchangeable as coins, as if love had nothing to do with the person who triggered it but you're the only one I look at and feel this jolt shaking my spine when you're near to me, and darling, when will that be?

The Number Before Infinity

5.   ∞

Skating Lessons

I tug my six-year-old around the rink,
shocked by the ice,
how it isolates each individual—
that yellow parka,
those blue mittens,
the red-knit cap
against a backdrop white
as a photographer's studio.

My daughter flows along
next to me, learning to skate
as I hold her hand. She tightens
her grip when she's frightened
her feet will go off on their own.
Our blades draw silver lines
that criss and cross each other.

Just yesterday I told her
I was leaving her mommy.
"How do you spell HATE?"
she asked me afterwards,
scribbling a note to me
on a scroll of register tape.

But today my daughter is really skating
at my side, taking her first shaky
steps on her own,
without holding my hand. She explains
how she'll do it:
"When you're near me I'll pretend
you're not here. When you're not here
I'll pretend you are."

Before-the-Divorce Rainboots

Shopping with my nine-year-old for rainboots,
she informs the saleslady, "Yellow
is the classic rain color." It's true
we want dazzle
on days of blue cloud.

I urge my daughter
toward the less expensive pair
but she won't let go
of the shiny ones.

And how can I refuse
when each morning my marriage sinks
a canto deeper into hell
and I'll soon be the braids of rain
on my daughter's window?

Beneath a Blue Moon

We kissed in your office
with the noon carillon
streaming over us.

On a chair facing yours, shorn
of fear, I sailed my fingers
across your cheek.

And that night
walking alone on the hill
above my house
I saw the lamps of the city
smoldering. The valley
where you live seemed
protected from the world
and by it
at the same time. Above me
the second full moon of this month
blued the sky
long into the night.

Departure at Chanukah

These are my last days in this house
where my first-born came home from the hospital
almost lost
in oversized red and white stripes,
where I poured banana pancakes
that the kids drenched in amber,
where the birthday girl and guests took turns
whacking a unicorn in the backyard
while I made the candy dance,
where my wife and I delved the weeds
that came back stronger each year.

These last nights
are also the final flames of the menorah,
the branches blooming with candles
as the stubby days burn down.

I'm leaving this house
wishing for a miracle,
a hope that will refresh itself
every year, like an oil lamp
that shines on and on
when no fuel could possibly be left. I'm searching
for an incendiary love.

The Number Before Infinity

6.   ∞

Dogsitting: Twelve Days

for John Martin and Diane Kirsten-Martin

Greta slumps shapeless on the sofa
by the window. She doesn't want to miss even one
instant of her owners' return, sleeping
in that spot each night.

By day her eyes pan across the outside
before she'll let me
hook on her leash, her tail
a question mark.
As much as she's yearning to walk
she hesitates,
worried
that her humans will slip back in
while she's out sampling
her grid of aromas.

Nights I walk her up and down each street,
past the stucco homes throbbing
with Christmas,
each of us alone
at our end of the leash,
waiting for a family.

Insomnia at the Solstice

Trapped in the longest night
I keep turning the key of sleep
but the engine stalls and stalls.
I long to snuggle your nape,
to nuzzle your cheek,
part the dark hairs that straggle
your brow. At the year's darkest hour
I behold a diadem of worries
and cry your name out loud.

Hilltop Townhouse

for Robert Thomas and Cheryl Morris

This house has a view
that verges on the airport
and at dusk
the sky is still giving up
its blue. The planes

dangle like sparklers
just above the runway—
a constellation
that yanked free from heaven
to burn on earth.

Flight 000

is the queasiness
when you're about to land
and you realize that this flight
with its snow mountain geodes
and its looking-glass lakes
this flight
which could have taken you anywhere
is actually going to drum down
in one certain city
where cars ghost along the artery
and families with wounded microwaves
and actual names sleep
in those dollhouses beyond the runway
and your life is not all lives
but only the best one
you can reach
in the time you have

1 BR Sublet ½-Frnshed

*It is not true that love makes all things easy:
it makes us choose what is difficult.*
—George Eliot, *Felix Holt, The Radical*

I'd rather be with you
in this apartment where the sofa breaks
when you think about sitting on it
and the electric coils of the stove
stay cold as snakes

Better here with you
than in any
white-on-white home

I'd rather stay with you—
though some of our friends don't
recognize us any more—
than pour out cool goblets during an evening
woven with guests

I want you

even if the hot water spits and curses
even if the electricity is narcoleptic
as Alice's Dormouse even if
I have to eat my morning granola
out of a teacup

I want your upside-down humor
your skein of deep brown hair
and your kisses
stoked with grief

Turquoise Planets of Your Eyes

I love to look at the turquoise planets of your eyes
and clench the furry tufts of your hair
and watch a smile billow across your face
and feel the scarves of your kisses
and shimmer my fingertips down your sides
read the Braille of your nipples
breeze just the hair of my arms along your belly
circumnavigate your clitoris
as you shift under the weight of your desire

and I love the hours afterwards
when our faces hover
barely apart
nuzzling
like sea lions
our lips
floating together
eyes seeking seeking eyes

those moments
when I have to remind myself
there are two of us

when I know
it will never be like this again

The Way We Touch

Our tongues have their own sign language.
Trade moist messages.
Our lips tremble together.

Through your blouse, your bra,
my mouth pulls shape
into your nipples,
speaking to them.

Sliding down, I can even taste you
through the last layer of clothing.
Finally I pull aside that cotton isthmus,
going to work—
a cat with a saucer of milk.
I fingerpaint you
outside and in.
Your knees gradually clench
around my shoulders
till I almost crack like a walnut.

And then it's your turn
to peel me
lick me slick me liquidly
pierce me
lap me up
the pleasure so knifed I hurl screams shudder my neck whinny
like a hippocampus laws of physics undulating
as my head comets through the wall of the sky

You're Not My Daddy

You're not my Daddy.
Your name's Mulligan
and you're a hobo without socks.

Listen, Mulligan.
I want you to hate me
and you're never coming to my wedding.

I know you only want to see me
so you won't have to pay Mommy as much.

I'm not renewing your contract, Daddy,
I'm returning you to the Daddy Store.

So stop loving me.
I'm fasting now,
fasting because I'm repenting
and I won't have any food
that's touched the table
where you eat with *her*.

I won't pay any attention to The Wind
when it talks to me
and says to look both ways before crossing.
Now I'm hitting The Wind.
Its hair is too short
like a sheep.

If I drop my backpack, Gravity will pick it up.
A Gravity Brown Sheep.
And if I'm too tired to walk any farther
the Gravity Brown Sheep will carry me
all the way home.

Rentals

The way a rental company
scans its cars
when they come home

circling each vehicle
inspecting for new nicks and scratches
they can charge me for

that's how she looks at the children
we made together
when I return them
to her safekeeping

The Number Before Infinity

7.

Outside the Borders

If I had lain awake all night
my heart crashing against my ribs
for thinking of you
and never leaped

If we had crammed this love into an affair
and I had known the clamor of your hair
only on those afternoons we hid away
like refugees pricking the border

if we had settled
only for that perfect
                        that horizontal
pas de deux

then I would never have known
last night's midnight birthday break
brut champagne and cursive cake
on the sofa our hearts
hiked up, exposed as a living wall
till we ate and drank it all

In Bed, With the Shade Up, on a Night in August

The moon is so near us tonight
that when you stretch up your hand
it lights
        on your finger
and you set it down
                trembling
on your white pillow

I Want You (To Start Taking Me More for Granted)

Don't worry that I'm going to fly
down the street after the first gossamer
that billows in my face—no,
I'm dinner on the table
when you get home.

I'm not going to jump
onto the next sail headed to Bora Bora
and Gauguin my way through the island girls—
none of them can do the puzzles
your tongue has solved.

I won't change the channel
to blondes or boys,
won't bet at roulette
your dark morning laugh.
I'm not about to slide back uphill to my ex.

I love how your hair is soft
as a fine watercolor brush
I can't resist
stroking my cheek with.

Indulgence

You say I should indulge myself
in baths turquoise with fragrant hops
that suede the skin

that I should tongue shadow-red wines
from vineyards stroked
by the autumns of Provence

that I should suck candies
that release the flavors
of tangerine and cassis

that I should froth my lips
with creamed and pressure-brewed beans
tended in forests of Sumatra and Zanzibar

that I should lie on sheets spun
only from the cocoons of silkworms
hand-fed with mulberry leaves

that I should stop lowering my body
to the hardwood floor
and pushing my face up till it drips

But I run so I can turn my heart
into a hand
that will hold you for decades

I indulge myself by licking
the pastilles of your chest
and the Shiraz in your goblet

I don't need any silk
except the skin nearest your ear—
the softest thing on earth—

and as for the baths
I'll step into them
if I can lie back

deep into your shoulder
and feel your wet fingers
rivering my hair

Modigliani and You

Modigliani is the only one who could paint
the bowls of your breasts,
the rise of your pelvis
when you half turn in bed,
those legs that stretch to the horizon,
and your Siamese-blue eyes. Only Modigliani
could catch on canvas
the smell of your skin,
the taste of your tongue.

But if he did your portrait
he'd probably try doing you,
the way he seduced Akhmatova
of the short black bangs
and the long gold scarf.

So let's skip Modigliani,
a Jewish boy from Livorno
who got knotted up in opium smoke,
and drowned in tuberculosis
at the end of Act One.

Tragedy's not our genre,
knock on wood. Let's hope
our lips will still clink
like champagne
till the final curtain rushes down.

Symmetron: You and Brother Will

                Shakespeare never got to see
  a Monet. Never gazed into liquid mirrors
          of the Seine.
         Yet he knew how to describe
a sateen shadow.
           He could speak beauty
             as well as anyone
                        who has a special ear
for the cool
     of a stream or the curves
              of a song.

         Someone could write a song
            about the curves
of your cool
      pomegranate lipstick, how a tongue awakens your ear.
  Sometimes it feels to this particular anyone
      as if your beauty
is part shadow,
     part the highest prime number. I need to describe
you, how you make me crazy and sane
                   as I look into your eye mirrors
   that Shakespeare was never lucky enough to see.

Exercise

No point in asking
where you learned to swash your tongue
that particular way
in just that spot

or who nibbled who
to teach you that magic trick
you perform with the clothes on

or how you figured out—
never mind.

All your ghost partners
hover behind you
and I can only thank them
for teaching you to dance so well.

A Sonnet — Against Regret

There are some years I'd love to toss behind
and even decades barbed with twists and ache,
so many scenes I'd just as soon rewind
if I could only roll another take—

I should have seen the storm that time carried
before I shingled my roof with half-lies,
should never in a million have married
until I sprouted my own set of eyes.

The short way, though, that led out of that scrape
was not a swift Euclidean line.
To reach this point, electric as Christmas,

I had to circle all around the cape
and sting my eyes with Magellanic brine
just to cross over a skinny isthmus.

Snarls

For a whole year after the separation
my daughter wouldn't let me brush her long brown hair

wouldn't let me stand behind her
and coax the tangles down
into the stories of the Sunday comics
as she spooned hot chocolate
topped with a whipped cream signature
released from the pressured can

For a whole year she refused
as if to say

You have caused me enough pain
and if you so much as yank one snarl
you will have done more
than I could forgive

Three Ages

> *I caress everything that was you*
> *in everything that's yet to be you*
> André Breton, *The Air of the Water*

When the sunlight prisms
your wild, dark hair
I see the blond days of your childhood
in the incandescent strands,

days when you ran
with your brothers and seven dogs
till the sun melted red,
and you finally stumbled indoors, your skin cooked,
your mother placing on your tongue
a cherry tomato she'd just picked.

But in those dark strands that I smooth,
strands the color of your coffee,
I see also clues
of the silver afternoons
when our faces will be books
and our hands will be valleys
and we'll take our grandchildren down to the ocean
to watch them wade.

Under a Black Lace Sky

After I've slid into the breakers of sleep
and you've reconciled your daughter to the dark
you step like a dancer back to our room
careful not to wake the floorboards

then you unhook the eyes of your bra
and glide into bed beside me

The domes of your breasts drape over me
pulling me out of my dream
and I wake to taste the confluence of our tongues
to smooth the coastline of your thigh

and I know
you and I were not meant to be Buddhas or saints
or tourists of the flesh

but to touch each other's fires
for so long as we can clasp one another
till the last strength
is lifted from our limbs

About the Author

Zack Rogow is the author, editor, or translator of twenty books and plays, including seven collections of poetry, three anthologies, four volumes of translation, and a children's book. He teaches in the graduate creative writing program at the University of Alaska, Anchorage. He is the editor of an anthology of U.S. poetry, *The Face of Poetry*, published by University of California Press. His translations of George Sand, Colette, and André Breton have won numerous awards, including the PEN/Book-of-the-Month Club Translation Award.

Also from Scarlet Tanager Books

Bone Strings by Anne Coray
    poetry, 80 pages, $15.00
Wild One by Lucille Lang Day
    poetry, 100 pages, $12.95
The "Fallen Western Star" Wars: A Debate About Literary California
edited by Jack Foley
    essays, 88 pages, $14.00
Catching the Bullet & Other Stories by Daniel Hawkes
    fiction, 64 pages, $12.95
Visions: Paintings Seen Through the Optic of Poetry
by Marc Elihu Hofstadter
    poetry, 72 pages, $14.00
Luck by Marc Elihu Hofstadter
    poetry, 104 pages, $16.00
Embrace by Risa Kaparo
    poetry, 70 pages, $14.00
red clay is talking by Naomi Ruth Lowinsky
    poetry, 142 pages, $14.95
crimes of the dreamer by Naomi Ruth Lowinsky
    poetry, 82 pages, $16.00
Everything Irish by Judy Wells
    poetry, 112 pages, $12.95
Call Home by Judy Wells
    poetry, 92 pages, $15.00
Turning a Train of Thought Upside Down: An Anthology of Women's Poetry
edited by Andrena Zawinksi
    poetry, 100 pages, $18.00

www.ingramcontent.com/pod-product-compliance
Lightning Source LLC
Chambersburg PA
CBHW032133090426
42743CB00007B/588